THE 12TH DAY OF

Christmas

Based on a heartwarming true story

KDP ISBN: 9781973391111
Imprint: Independently published by Sego Publishing LLC.

THE 12TH DAY OF

Christmas

Based on a heartwarming true story

June Standley

God does notice us, and he watches over us. But it is usually through another person that he meets our needs.

—*Spencer W. Kimball*

CHAPTER ONE

Jenna slammed the front door behind her with such force it catapulted the Christmas wreath into the snow—a fir-bough and red-ribbon heap of Christmas cheer.

Ice crystals flew everywhere as she stomped down into the wood entry way to the hall closet where she let her purse drop to the floor with a dull, satisfying thud. Yanking off her coat, she opened the closet door and stuffed it in without bothering to put it on a hanger. Despite her mood, she couldn't suppress a wry smile. At twenty-eight, it wasn't often she got to throw a temper-tantrum—even a small one—and she'd forgotten how truly satisfying it felt.

"I'm home." Jenna huffed, as she tried to bend past her pregnant belly to unlace her boot.

"Oh, really?" Nick answered in mock surprise from the kitchen. "I didn't hear you storm in!" Nick added with a laugh as he finished pouring milk into steaming bowls of oatmeal for five-year-old Emily and three-year-old Matt.

"Hi Mommy!" the children called in unison.

"Hi guys," Jenna called back as she stepped out of her boot—and right into a puddle of melted snow. "Nice, Jenna," she grumbled to herself, pulling off her soggy sock to drape over the door handle. She tried to use her bare toes to anchor her other boot and pull it off, but it just wouldn't budge. Grabbing the boot with both hands she began to awkwardly hop around as she struggled to pull it off. Suddenly she slipped and lurched backward into the wall, her booted foot coming down hard on the floor.

"Are you okay?" Nick asked, hurrying from the kitchen.

"Yeah, I'm fine," Jenna frowned.

"Here, let me help you with that." He gave her a quick hug and peck on the cheek before bending down to help with the boot.

"Thanks, Honey" she sighed, slightly winded.

Jenna leaned heavily against the wall while Nick worked at her laces. "There. I think that ought to do it," he announced in a moment with a smile. "By the way, how did your meeting go at the church this morning? Did you get your assignment for the Twelve Days of Christmas?"

"Yeah, I got it," Jenna sighed, shaking her head. For reasons she could barely fathom now, she had volunteered in church to participate in a Christmas service project.

Recently, their pastor had explained that he had identified two individuals from their local community who needed additional help this Christmas. He proposed a service project to fill their needs. The idea was to have someone bring a gift every night to each individual on the twelve days leading up to Christmas. He was calling it, "The Twelve Days of

Christmas," and invited his congregation to provide Christmas gifts to a young, single girl who had just given birth to twins and an elderly woman who was nearly blind and housebound because of arthritis.

Thinking about it now, Jenna really didn't know what possessed her to sign up. After all, she was already bone-tired with her pregnancy and she certainly didn't need something else to sap at her energy. That's what she had been trying to convince herself of, anyway. But the fact of the matter was she was a little worried about herself. Not physically speaking—Aside from feeling tired most of the time, she felt fine that way. No, it was something else. For the past several weeks she had been feeling so…Christmas Spirit-less, maybe? Was that even a thing?

Whatever the reason, the "season of comfort and joy" seemed anything but that to Jenna right now. Maybe it wasn't that big of a deal to anyone else, but to Jenna it was a concern. She'd always looked forward to Christmas and enjoyed everything about the holiday season. But not this year. She felt off and she didn't like it. Hoping for a change, something to get past the dullness she felt, Jenna had made her concern part of her prayers—but honestly, lately it seemed like even her prayers were lackluster.

When Becky, Jenna's women's leader at church, announced she was sending around the sign-up list for The Twelve Days of Christmas project, Jenna was surprised to feel a spark of excitement flicker to life inside her. At the same moment, suddenly one childhood memory after another paraded through her mind: Her mom baking homemade chocolate chip cookies for a new neighbor. Her dad helping friends with their car. Both her parents going to visit a sick acquaintance. Jenna's mom again, caring for a neighbor's children so she could rest after a new baby. As these memories marched past, a passage of scripture from The New Testament came to mind. "For whosoever will save his life shall lose it: but whosoever will lose his life for my sake, the same shall save it."

As Jenna pondered this unexpected thought, it dawned on her right there in the middle of church, that maybe the answer to her prayers; the answer to her cheerlessness, was service! Just as she caught hold of that thought, she recalled a partial sermon which blossomed in her mind: her pastor had told his congregation that unless they lost themselves in service to others like the Savior had, there was little purpose to their own lives. Further, those who live only for themselves would eventually shrivel spiritually, while those who lose themselves in service to others would find life happy and full— and in effect save their lives.

Jenna's whole soul seemed to catch fire as she considered these new thoughts. She didn't know why she hadn't taken much notice of her pastor's words before. But now, she felt certain that if she could extend herself to someone, she'd find the Christmas Spirit she was looking for. Not only that, but maybe in the process, she could be a blessing in someone else's life.

When the woman sitting next to Jenna had

handed her the sign-up sheet, Jenna smiled as she wrote her name on the list—she even added a little note saying how much she'd like to help the young mother. After all, she figured they probably had a lot in common.

Happily, (amazingly) over the next several days, Jenna had made plans for the new little family as she anxiously awaited confirmation of her assignment the coming Saturday. While she waited, she imagined the gifts she would give each of the twins and the new mother. Thoughts of beautiful little clothes, warm blankets and cute baby toys filled her head. It was amazing to her how great it felt to be thinking about someone else other than herself and her own family.

The week passed slowly, but finally Saturday morning arrived. The Twelve Days of Christmas volunteers were supposed to meet at the church and get their assignments. Jenna was anxious to find out what the little family needed and then start shopping.

The church was only a couple blocks away, so she bundled up and with a bounce in her step, set out into the bright, clear winter morning. Arriving at the church, Jenna hastily stomped the snow off her boots and stepped inside, grateful for the sudden warmth. She could hear a low murmur of voices and smell the delicious scent of hot chocolate and warm homemade cinnamon rolls wafting from the large gathering room down the hall. As Jenna entered, Becky approached with a smile and a hug.

"Thanks so much for helping with the project; I know you've got a lot going on with the baby

coming and all, but we're grateful for your help."
Jenna smiled and warmly responded, "Oh, no
worries, I'm actually really excited about it! It seems
like such a fun idea."

"I'm so glad to hear it. So—have you checked
the bulletin board yet for your assignment?" Becky
asked, nodding toward the back of the room. "I
posted everyone's assignment there. You'll want to
grab a notecard from the table too. It will have the
address of the person you're assigned on it."

Jenna thanked Becky and headed for the back
of the room where a group was gathered. The
Twelve Days of Christmas assignments were listed
on two sheets of paper. Jenna anxiously scanned
the first paper and found her name at the bottom.
Jenna's excitement mounted as she saw that she was
assigned the very last day of gift giving—the twelfth
day, which would be on Christmas Eve.

She was thrilled! Now that she knew what day
she was assigned, she glanced up at the top of the
sheet to put a name to the face she had been imag-
ining for the past few weeks. Ah, there it was. The
young woman's name was Evaletta Larson.

Jenna's brow furrowed momentarily as she
wondered why the names of the twins weren't listed.
She'd hoped to know their names, so she could put
tags on their gifts. Jenna scanned the sheet again.
Not seeing the twin's names, she glanced at the
adjacent assignment sheet tacked to the board—
and her eyes widened in dismay. There at the top of
the second sheet of paper she could plainly see the
names of the young mother and her two children.

Jenna's heart sank in realization: she had been assigned to the old woman, not the young mother and the babies.

Jenna felt a sharp pang of disappointment. Turning, she anxiously scanned the crowd for Becky. She was near the exit, saying her good-byes to several women who were leaving. Jenna quickly made her way across the room and waited anxiously for the conversation to finish before approaching. "Hey Becky?" she said, trying to feign a casualness she didn't feel.

Her friend turned to her with a warm smile. "So, you found your assignment. Are you excited?" She asked, expectantly.

Taking a deep breath to steady herself, Jenna hesitated. "Well, yes, but . . ." she glanced to the floor, trying to decide how best to put her dilemma to words.

"What is it?" Becky asked, gently.

Jenna decided to just plow ahead: "Well, I think there may be some kind of mistake."

She looked up at Becky, whose eyes widened slightly but other than that her expression didn't change.

"A mistake?" she repeated. "What do you mean?"

Jenna felt her cheeks flush and she glanced away again under Becky's steady gaze. She knew she couldn't let the moment pass though, so she forced her eyes back to Becky's. "Well, it looks like I've been assigned to the elderly woman."

"Yes?" Becky nodded, encouraging Jenna to continue.

"Well, actually, I signed up to help with the young mother and the twins. I even made a note on the sign-up list. I just thought I could relate best to her as a young mother myself."

"And?"

"And, well, I don't mean to make a big deal about this, but—" this was getting messier than Jenna imagined. All she needed for Becky to do was switch her name. She didn't want to have to confess to Becky that she became very anxious when she was around the elderly, but she didn't know what else she could say to make her change the assignment.

"I . . . I just don't do well around old people and I really don't think this assignment is going to work out. Can't you just switch my name and put me on the other list?" Jenna's eyes dropped to the floor again and her cheeks burned even brighter at what she imagined Becky must be thinking.

Becky gently slipped her arm through Jenna's. "Hey, why don't we sit down for a sec, ok?" She led Jenna to a quiet corner where they sat down to talk—well, mostly Becky talked. Jenna sat staring at the floor and listened. Becky encouraged her to go ahead with Evaletta, telling her that maybe there were unexpected blessings in it for her, and that she'd enjoy getting to know her. Sighing, Jenna agreed that certainly was possible—but to herself she thought that it wasn't likely.

The beauty of the brisk, bright day was lost on Jenna as she made her way home. As she trudged through the snow, she kept turning things over in her head. The more she thought about her assignment, the more irritable she felt. Hadn't God seen how willing she was to help the young mother and her babies? Didn't He realize she was looking for ways to feel the Spirit of Christmas? Then why, for Heaven's sake, was she assigned to the elderly woman?

CHAPTER TWO

"It really doesn't matter now who I am assigned to." Jenna answered Nick with an exaggerated shrug. "I decided on the way home that I'm not going to do the Twelve Days of Christmas." Then, seeing the look of dismay on Nick's face she knew would be there, she hastily added, "I really don't have the time—you know how tired I've felt and how busy it is this time of year." Jenna looked at Nick for support. His face was still registering disbelief, so she hurriedly continued, "and I've got more free-lance work than I can handle. And, you know, with caring for the children and keeping up the house, and this new baby . . ." she trailed off. Jenna's excuses sounded shallow and lame even to her.

Nick's sea-blue eyes were searching Jenna's as he tried to read between her lines. He knew she'd been excited about the service project before she left for her meeting. "But you seemed really happy about doing this ever since you heard about it. And didn't you say this was the perfect way for you to feel more of the Christmas Spirit?"

"I did," Jenna frowned, sighing heavily. "But I didn't know when I agreed to do this that I was going to be assigned to some little old blind lady!"

she exclaimed.

She could see the lights click on in Nick's head. He tried to suppress a smile, but she knew exactly what he was thinking: Jenna Goodman had been assigned to help an old woman—how ironic was that? The only person he knew in the entire world that was completely intimidated by the elderly, and she'd been assigned to help one at Christmas.

"Come here." He said, gently taking hold of one of Jenna's hands, his eyes twinkling with amusement.

"No, you're laughing at me." she pouted.

"I'm not laughing." Nick replied softly, as he slowly pulled her closer. "I'm just smiling because I just find it an interesting predicament, that's all."

"What? I can't help it if old people scare me!" Jenna said defensively.

"I know, Honey," Nick said, as he wrapped his arms around her.

Reluctantly she laid her head on his broad shoulder. Her fingers automatically found the back of his neck and curled themselves up in his thick brown hair as she thought about how she'd come to acquire such an irrational fear.

Jenna knew exactly when it had started: she was just five years old when her mother had brought her widowed grandmother home to care for her through the last stages of cancer. Her Grandma lived so far away, she'd never actually met her before. All she knew was that she had to give up her bedroom and her bed for a pale, sick, old woman—and sleep in her older sister's room. The moans of pain that emanated from Jenna's bedroom scared her to death.

She didn't dare go near her bedroom, not even to get her toys.

She remembered her mother kept a loving and patient vigil by her mother's bedside night and day for more than two months. Whenever Jenna worked up enough courage to peek through the crack of the partially open door her mom shooed her away. Then one day, it was over. Jenna's grandmother had died, and she had died in her bed. It still gave her chills to even think about it.

Years passed before Jenna had any significant contact again with anyone older than her parents. She was 14 when her mother volunteered her to help a friend with the elderly ladies she cared for in her home. Mrs. Rogers thought a nice trip to the State Fair was just what her usually home-bound wards needed, but she was short on help. All Jenna was supposed to do was push one of the wheel chairs around the fair, help the elderly ladies get some air, and that was it.

Reluctantly Jenna had agreed to do it, and admittedly, things were just fine—until the senile lady she was pushing begged her to stop in front of a 4-H display of pigs. A small group of people had gathered around the low wooden pen to watch a fat sow nursing a scrambling horde of pink little piglets.

Jenna stopped the wheelchair and had only been watching the pigs for a moment when suddenly the old lady lurched out of the chair and, with out-stretched arms, started shouting, "Here kitty-kitty! Here kitty-kitty!" Before she knew what was happening, the old woman was leaning over the short fence, exposing her under clothes to the world, and trying to grab one of the little piglets. That of course caused havoc in the pen and piglets went squealing and running everywhere.

Jenna was so shocked at the sudden turn of events she couldn't move for a moment. But then she bolted into action when she realized the angry sow was going to charge the old woman leaning over the fence. Jenna tried everything she could to get the woman to step back. She even wrapped her skinny arms around the only thing she could grab on to—the elderly woman's ample hips—and tried to pull her away, but to no avail. By then the sow was up and in motion and a moment later she plowed into the old lady just as the woman snatched up a squealing piglet.

Fortunately, the fence absorbed most of the shock of the charge, but still, the big sow succeeded in toppling the old woman backwards. The old woman, the piglet and Jenna tumbled to the hard-packed dirt in a melee of hooves, arms and legs.

The impact of the fall had bounced the "kitten" right out of the arms of the old woman, leaving the terrified piglet trembling with fright only an arm's length away from her. The old woman began crawling toward the piglet cooing, "Here kitty-kitty," until she was close enough to pull the animal into her arms again. Then she promptly sat on the ground and began stroking the piglet while rocking back and forth, oblivious to the rather large crowd of very amused spectators that had gathered around.

The fall had knocked the wind out of Jenna, but

Mrs. Rogers was there to help her to her feet and dust her off. Jenna must have hit her head hard because she had a terrible headache. Her tail bone felt bruised, and her elbow was cut and bleeding. What a mess!

Jenna couldn't believe what had happened—was happening. Her cheeks were burning bright with embarrassment and it was all she could do to ignore the crowd and help Mrs. Rogers coax the old woman into letting go of the "kitten", and sitting back down in the wheel chair.

It was then that Jenna vowed she would NEVER go near another old person as long as she lived! And frankly, she could say she'd been pretty successful on that particular point. But now—

Jenna pulled away from Nick far enough to see his face. "After I saw my assignment, I tried to tell Becky I wanted to switch the names—you know how I was hoping to get the new mom and her babies—but I couldn't get Becky to understand. She told me she felt it would work out with the old woman and that it just might prove to be a blessing." Jenna shook her head incredulously. "Oh Nick," she said, looking a little sheepish. "I know you must think I sound so awful and selfish, but I just can't do this! This is stressing me out so much, I really can't."

"Sure you can," Nick soothed as he gathered Jenna into his arms again. "It will be fine. You'll see."

Maybe he thought so, but Jenna was harboring some serious doubts.

CHAPTER THREE

That evening, Evaletta Larson paused in her chores, her dust cloth poised above the cherry wood end table she was working on in her living room. She glanced up at the big picture window in the adjoining dining room where golden shafts of sunlight had suddenly appeared, brightening the room in the sudden glow. There were few things Evaletta enjoyed more than a beautiful sunset— and winter sunsets always seemed to be the most brilliant. With a burst of girlish excitement that belied her eighty-six-year-old body, Evaletta dropped her dust cloth and hurried as fast as her walker would allow her to the big picture window.

The sunset was breathtaking. It was as if the sun was heralding a glorious victory over the gray, dismal day with reckless abandon: Rich purples tumbled into crimson reds and blended with brilliant oranges, beautiful pinks, bright yellows and every other color and hue in between. It was magnificent!

For a brief moment, the colors of the sunset seemed to intensify even more and then they began to slowly fade. Evaletta closed her eyes, and as she did so, memories flooded into her mind unbidden, but welcome. It was here in this place that she had stood so many times before with her late husband Richard. They would stand together, arms wrapped around each other, her head tucked under his chin as they watched the sun sink in the sky. A faint smile passed across Evaletta's deeply creased face as she thought of him. If he were there with her now, he would have gently lifted her chin with his fingers, like he had done so many times before, and then look deeply into her eyes for a moment before tenderly saying, "I dedicate this sunset to you, my love."

Evaletta sighed forlornly and reluctantly opened her pale blue eyes. She didn't want to let go of the memory quite yet, but the sun was almost gone now, and the dark December night was beginning to gather in. Evaletta involuntarily shivered as she watched the last bit of color drain from the sky like water colors on a wet canvas.

She leaned heavily on her walker and sighed. Another day had passed. One more day without Richard, her dear, sweet companion of sixty-two years. With an almost imperceptible shake of her head, Evaletta slowly turned and made her way back toward her quiet, lonely living room.

The night was still young, and much could probably be accomplished before going to bed, but Evaletta didn't feel like accomplishing much tonight. She was tired after a long day of cleaning house. It took a lot of effort to sweep, polish and wipe things down, especially with a walker in tow. Now her arthritic hips and knees protested her activity with pain and swelling. She was tempted to finish dusting the end table just to be done with it, but she realized all she really wanted to do was get off her feet and rest for a bit.

As Evaletta hobbled toward her favorite chair she stopped in front of a large black and white photo that hung over the narrow writing desk between the dining room and the living room. It was a grand picture of Richard. Her favorite.

She clearly remembered the day the picture was taken more than forty years ago. Their teen-aged son, James, was a budding photographer then, and as usual had his camera around his neck. Richard had just come home from work as an insurance salesman and had finished telling them about a funny incident that had them all in stitches. James had captured forever a profile image of his dad laughing uproariously. Richard's head was thrown back in a huge laugh that tilted his fedora hat backwards at a precarious angle. The top button of his white shirt was undone under his dark suit jacket and the knot of his tie hung loose around his neck. His eyes sparkled with the delight of someone who loved to laugh. The picture was perfect.

The memory of that day made Evaletta smile. Those were such good times. A house full of children, meals to cook, activities to attend to. And Richard. Evaletta blinked back the familiar moisture that began to gather in her eyes. It had been more than three years since Richard had unexpectedly slipped away in his sleep, but to Evaletta the pain of his loss was still deep, still fresh and sometimes still unbearable.

Evaletta lifted her thick glasses and dabbed at her eyes with a tissue from the box she kept on the desk. Then she resolutely took a deep breath and straightened her shoulders. It had always distressed Richard to see her cry, and she was self-conscious of her tears.

"I'm sorry Richard," she murmured to the photo. "I didn't mean to cry again in front of you." Evaletta studied the handsome features of Richard's face a moment longer. Then she turned and continued to the overstuffed wingback in front of the television, her vision blurred by the moisture in her eyes. She slowly lowered herself onto the cushioned seat; her arthritic knees and hips protesting the strain. She couldn't help but sigh—oh, but it felt good to sit down.

She found the remote control and turned on the TV. The bluish-white light of the screen flickered for a moment and then came on, the only illumination in the otherwise dim room. The monotone of the evening news cast hummed quietly. Settling into the chair, Evaletta leaned her head back, took off her glasses and closed her eyes. Time lost all meaning. Evaletta's thoughts automatically turned to her husband and she let them run, unchecked. Richard—dashingly handsome—deep blue eyes and a shock of thick, dark hair—devastating smile—first time she saw him he flashed her that smile—making her heart skip a beat—she was cleaning up the tables in the lunch room at the college becasue she needed the extra income—he dropped his fork on purpose—asked for a clean one—asked her name—she couldn't believe someone so popular, so handsome wanted to know her—asked her to the dance—danced all night—on cloud nine—soon they were seeing each other whenever they could—went on lots of long walks together along the river—took her in his arms for the first time—strong, safe—asked if he could kiss her—his lips, soft, warm, tender—her heart pounding—stars glittering, moon shining—knew she wanted to be with him forever.

Tears slipped from Evaletta's closed eyes and found downward paths in the network of wrinkles that creased her face. "Oh Sweetheart." She breathed, her voice barely audible. "Do you think of me as often as I think of you?" Evaletta sighed, "My darling . . . *do you still love me?*"

The question hung in the dark room like an impenetrable fog. Dense, cold and shadowy, it was far too formidable to navigate and too big to simply ignore. By sheer force of will, Evaletta opened her eyes, hoping that the physical movement would somehow dispel the black clouds of anguish that, over the last couple of months, had insidiously crept into her consciousness to grow and fester until it clouded her every moment, every thought. An involuntary shudder ran up her spine. Why did she have such terrible thoughts? There was no reason to doubt her husband's love in life, so why was there doubt in death? Still . . .

Unable to stop the flow of tears she knew would be coming, Evaletta gave into it and openly wept, her shoulders shuddering with each sob. It took several minutes for Evaletta to compose herself, but finally the tears stopped. With great effort, she hauled herself up from the chair to get a fresh tissue from the box on the desk. She looked at Richard's photo one more time, and then she closed her eyes in prayer.

"O Father in Heaven," she whispered, "I am so grateful unto Thee for the blessings that I have, which I know are many. But there is one more blessing that I want—that I desperately need! Won't you please listen to the pleas of an old woman and answer my prayers?"

CHAPTER FOUR

"Mo-om!" Emily wailed from the family room where she was sitting on the floor with a box of markers. "Matty won't give me back my Christmas book!"

"It mine!" Matt declared defiantly, hugging the gift catalog close to his chest with his skinny little arms.

"No, it's not!" Emily shouted as she got to her knees to try to pull the book away from her stubborn little brother. "I had it first!"

"Children! Please stop fighting!" Jenna wearily called from the kitchen sink where she was preparing a salad to go with their dinner. It was more a plea than a command.

"But Mom!" Emily loudly protested, "I was marking the things I want Santa to bring me for Christmas when he took the book away from me!"

Jenna closed her eyes for a moment and took a deep breath. How in the world was she supposed to make progress with dinner if she had to stop what she was doing every three minutes to referee?

Jenna looked at her tired face in the dark reflection of the window over the sink. It had been a long day and it showed. It certainly wasn't easy running a

31

business out of her home and caring for house and family at the same time, especially now that Emily was on Christmas vacation. Thankfully the kids usually played well together, and that helped a little.

"Mommy!" This time it was Matt. Jenna picked up a kitchen towel and dried her hands before walking into the family room.

"Okay you two, I've about had it with the Christmas catalogue. Since you are both fighting over it, neither one of you gets it right now." Jenna gently pulled the book from Matt's reluctant hands and put it on top of the fridge. "Besides, if you want to go Christmas shopping tonight, we need to get dinner quickly—and that means I need help setting the table," she added, looking directly at her daughter.

"No, that's not fair!" Emily pouted as she folded her arms and glared at her mother. "Why do I always have to set the table and Matty doesn't do anything?" she demanded.

"Because young lady," Jenna patiently explained, "you are big enough to help and Matt isn't yet."

"I a big boy, Mommy." Matt declared solemnly, standing up to his full three-year old stature. Jenna had to smile.

"Well, look at you! You are getting to be a big boy, aren't you?" she said and patted her little boy's curly blonde head. "Do you want to help Emily set the table?" she asked. Matt nodded his head vigorously. "Okay then," she said, "Emily will let you put the spoons on the table. Is that okay?" Jenna asked looking at both. They nodded their heads. "All right" she said, gently swatting Matt's behind, "let's go get the table set."

Jenna turned back to the salad as the children gathered the table settings. "Oh, I almost forgot to tell you something Mom!" Emily exclaimed.

"What's that, honey?" Jenna smiled, looking up at her daughter from the carrot she was peeling. From her dark brown hair to her smooth skin and blue eyes, Emily looked so much like her father, their relationship was unmistakable.

"I saw the perfect present for the old lady you're supposed to visit!" Emily announced with obvious pride in her accomplishment.

Jenna felt a familiar pit form in her stomach. Oh no, not the elderly woman again. Ever since she got her assignment the children had been curious about Evaletta. Every day was a new question: How old was she? What did she look like? Did she have white hair or blue like old Mrs. Hampton at church? How come old people have wrinkles? When was she going to go see her? What gift was she going to give her? Frankly Jenna was tired of thinking about it.

Jenna couldn't even think about Christmas now without feeling unsettled. She had been trying, rather unsuccessfully, to push aside all the guilt she now associated with The Twelve Days of Christmas service project.

Today would have been the first day of gift giving. Even though a week had passed since she'd received her assignment, and despite Nick's encouragement, Jenna was still determined not to participate. She really didn't need that in her life. She had plenty on her plate to keep her busy. Besides, now she felt genuinely tired and her own Christmas preparations still needed attention. So much for trying to feel more of the Spirit of Christmas like she wanted to. It was about all she could do to just get through each day.

And honestly, what was one more gift to a little old lady that probably had everything anyway? What could Jenna possibly offer her that she didn't already have? Jenna sighed and turned to Emily. "What gift would be perfect for the old lady?" she asked Emily as patiently as she could.

"I saw it on TV. It's wrinkle remover!" Emily said, nodding enthusiastically. "The lady on TV said it can make you look ten-years younger! I bet the old lady would like that, wouldn't she?"

"She probably would." Jenna agreed with a chuckle. "I'll have to keep that in mind."

A few minutes later Nick walked through the door, his coat and briefcase in hand. The children ran to meet him. He put his things down on the end of the sofa just in time to catch them both up in a big daddy hug and spin them around before he put the giggling duo down. He smiled and winked at Jenna before sitting with the kids for a minute to hear about their day.

Jenna watched the nightly ritual with deep and tender satisfaction. It was funny looking back on it now. She had fallen in love with Nick because of his rugged good-looks and for all the other romantic reasons people get married. But during our court-ship she hadn't really considered what kind of father he might be. To her pleasant surprise, Nick took to fatherhood naturally and absolutely adored their children. And she loved him even more because of it.

"Okay guys," Nick said as he lowered Matt off his lap to the floor, "why don't you two go and play for a minute while I say hello to your mother."

Nick smiled broadly at Jenna as he leaned over her tummy to embrace her and place a lingering kiss on her mouth followed by another shorter kiss. She smiled back at him. He always kissed her like that. It was his trademark from the very beginning.

"Hi Sweetheart," he said tenderly, aware of the fatigue that showed in her eyes. "How are you feeling?"

"I'm good," Jenna answered. "Maybe a bit tired though." She leaned her head on his shoulder a moment and closed her eyes. It was nice to be held after such a hectic day. "How was work for you?" she murmured into his shoulder.

"Just fine," said Nick. "I can tell you about it later. Are you still feeling up to shopping tonight?"

"Yes," Jenna said, taking a deep breath and straightening up. "The children are excited about it and we have dinner ready now, so we can eat and go."

"Great," said Nick enthusiastically, "I'm starved!

CHAPTER FIVE

Just a few blocks away, Evaletta shuffled into the living room behind her walker. She paused for a moment to gaze at Richard's picture before continuing to the living room.

Settling into her chair Evaletta removed her glasses and leaned her head back on the overstuffed chair. The day had been long, and she was bone-tired, but not quite sleepy yet.

Suddenly the doorbell rang, startling Evaletta so much she involuntarily jumped and spilled her glasses from her lap. They fell to the floor, bounced once and came to rest under the sofa.

Evaletta was frozen with indecision: answer the door or try to find her glasses. She wasn't expecting anyone, especially after dark, and she hesitated to answer the door. Besides, she had just sat down and her knees seemed worse than ever tonight, and it would make getting up again a painful and slow process. But who was at her door? After a moment, Evaletta's curiosity got the best of her. Her glasses could wait for her, whoever was at the door might not.

She wrapped the crocheted lap blanket she kept on the arm of the chair around her shoulders, then slowly, painfully pulled herself to her feet. She shuffled the walker as quickly as she could across the room.

Evaletta opened the door. "Hello?" she said expectantly. "Hello? Is anybody there?" she asked, opening the storm door and peering outside. A frigid blast of winter made her shudder, but it didn't stop her. She stepped out onto the porch and squinted into the night, thinking that whoever had rung the bell had gotten tired of waiting and might still be nearby. She glanced to the right and left, but seeing no one, she turned to go back inside. Just then her foot touched something. It appeared to be a small package. With great effort, Evaletta bent down and picked it up. "Well, what have we here?" she said as she examined the gift. It was a small box wrapped in Christmas paper with a typed note on the top. Evaletta looked around again, but without her glasses, she was nearly blind.

Standing under the bright porch light, Evaletta held the package so close to her face that the note nearly touched her nose. She could just barely make out what it said:

On the first day of Christmas
We wanted to find a way
To bring more cheer to your heart
And to start your holiday.

The note went on to say that she could expect 11 more gifts over the next eleven days from various individuals, and that they might be delivered anonymously or in person.

"Oh, my word!" Evaletta exclaimed when she

finished reading the note, thinking how much fun it would be to have so many visitors.

Evaletta carefully put the gift in the wire basket attached to her walker, closed the door and shuffled her way back to her chair. She scanned the floor for her glasses, but it was useless. She could see nothing. Thinking it might be better to try to find her glasses in the morning when the light of day would brighten the room, she lowered herself once again into her chair.

After getting comfortable once again, she retrieved the gift from her basket. "Well you little rascal, you've caused a lot of havoc around her tonight!" she exclaimed. She turned the small box around and around, savoring the beauty of the wrapping. "Can you believe it old girl?" She asked herself after a moment. "Someone was thinking of you today. Imagine that! And they brought you a gift!" Her hands trembled with excitement as she carefully removed the paper. Inside the small box she found a beautiful handkerchief edged with a delicate hand-crocheted lace. "Evaletta" was ornately embroidered into the fine cloth with an elegant Christmas motif.

At that moment, the world stopped for Evaletta. It was as if she had been given a small break from her pain and loneliness, and she burst into tears at the unexpected thoughtfulness of someone else. The gift lifted her soul in a way she didn't think was possible anymore.

CHAPTER SIX

As Jenna lay in bed early on the morning of the Eleventh Day of Christmas, her thoughts turned to the old woman she was supposed to visit the next day. Despite her best efforts to stay blissfully occupied over the previous days, she was beginning to feel the uncomfortable pricks of a guilty conscience.

After all, she had been looking for opportunities to help others. And she had signed up to help—no one had forced her to do that. And it wasn't like it was the old woman's fault that Jenna had been assigned to her.

An hour later as she was helping Nick get ready for work she had finally come to a decision. She had decided that she would do her part and bring a gift to Evaletta Larson for the twelfth day of Christmas. As Jenna handed Nick his lunch bag, she shyly looked at him and said, "So, I think I just might do the Twelve Days of Christmas, after all."

Nick's surprise showed in his face, but Jenna could see he was also pleased. "That's great news, Honey," Nick smiled reassuringly. "I'm happy for you—and I'm sure Mrs. Larson will be just as pleased."

"Thanks. I just don't know what to get her. She

probably has everything she needs."

"Well then, how about chocolate or Christmas cookies?" Nick responded as he gathered his coat and keys.

"Hmm, she might be diabetic." Jenna replied.

"Slippers, or maybe a blouse?"

"I don't know what size she wears," Jenna answered glumly.

"Oh. Well, what about a heating pad?" Nick suggested.

"Way too boring." Jenna countered.

"Scarf and mittens?" He tried one last time.

"She probably already has those." Jenna answered with a sigh, plopping down on the sofa. "Sorry to shoot down all your ideas," she said sheepishly.

"You don't have to apologize, honey. I know it's been tough." Nick said gently, setting his things down and taking a moment to sit next to Jenna on the sofa. Pulling her close he added, "Look, as far as the gift goes, maybe if you just try and keep it simple, it won't matter so much what it is. It might just be the thought that counts to her. As far as everything else, we're a team, remember? I know you're tired, so let me help more with the kids and meals. I'm sure we can get through all of this together, ok?"

"Okay," Jenna sighed. "I'll give some more thought to the gift. Maybe when you get home from work tonight, I can run to the store."

"Okay Hon. I'd better go, or I'll be late." Nick kissed Jenna and headed out the door. "Love you.

See you tonight."

"Love you too."

When evening came, Nick surprised the family by coming home from work a little earlier than expected. They decided it might be fun to go out for burgers with the children and then look at some of the Christmas lights around town. However, by the time they got home it was later than Jenna had anticipated, and the stores were closed.

Nick was already asleep by the time Jenna got ready for bed that night. The children were a little more rambunctious than usual and it took a while to quiet them down and settle them in.

As Jenna quietly changed into her pajamas, her thoughts drifted from the kids to the things she had wanted to accomplish that day, but hadn't. One of those things was getting a gift for Evaletta Larson. Jenna felt almost physically ill with guilt for having not made it to the store. What was she going to do? She was supposed to give her gift tomorrow evening and she had nothing. Jenna sighed and shook her head. Why had this whole experience been so hard? Why wasn't she assigned to the new mom and her babies? She would have loved that! But no, instead she was assigned to an old woman who could barely see, let alone walk. What do you get for someone like that?

Jenna gently pulled back the comforter and slipped as quietly as she could into bed beside Nick. She stared at the ceiling, trying to will sleep to come, but feeling anxious about the next day. Maybe she was better off not giving the gift after all, she wondered as she turned to her side and snuggled the thick, warm blankets around her. No one would know she didn't do it besides herself—and Mrs. Larson.

Jenna closed her eyes and finally drifted off to sleep, still wondering if she could ignore the Twelfth Day of Christmas. As she slept, she dreamed she was living in a small, cold house, and it surprised her to discover that she was old and frail. Her belongings were meager and her visitors were few, but tonight she was happy because it was Christmas Eve and she was expecting a visitor. She didn't know who it could be because her family was long gone and she was mostly forgotten by anyone who knew her. Still, the thought of having someone come to visit, especially this night, was thrilling. Jenna puttered around all day tidying up as best as she could. She wished she had something to give her visitor to express her gratitude, but there was nothing that could be easily spared, and she hoped they would understand.

Finally, as evening fell, Jenna eased herself into her rocking chair and settled in to wait. Every sound from the street seemed to reach her ears as she listened anxiously for someone to come up the walk. The minutes slipped by. Slowly the minutes turned into hours. Still no one came. The chill of the night crept into the house while doubt, cold and pervasive, slipped into Jenna's heart. Finally, acknowledging that it was too late for anyone to come, a sharp disappointment swelled her heart to breaking, and a flood of tears spilled from her eyes.

Abruptly, Jenna awoke and for a moment or two, she was disoriented. The dream had felt so real. She realized her cheeks were wet with tears, and when she wiped her face the relief she felt from touching the youthful smoothness of her skin, almost made her cry again.

Jenna was anxious to go back to sleep, but she couldn't shake the deep sorrow she felt from the dream. Settling back under the blankets, Jenna listened to Nick's rhythmic breathing next to her. How grateful she was to still be young and surrounded by a loving family! She had Nick and Emily and Matt. She had a new baby growing inside her. She had friends and extended family. As Jenna lay there thinking about the dream and the blessings she enjoyed, thoughts of Evaletta came forcefully to mind. She was old. She was widowed. She was alone. She was blind and sick.

Jenna was immediately consumed with over-whelming guilt. How calloused and selfish she had been! How terrible of her to not want to help a lonely old woman, and at Christmas time no less. What had she been thinking? A fresh wave of tears, this time of heart-felt remorse, slipped down her cheeks to the pillow below. "Oh, Dear God", she prayed, "please forgive me and help me show kindness to this lonely old woman."

CHAPTER SEVEN

Saturday, December 24th dawned cold and snowy, but despite the weather, Jenna woke up with a new sense of excitement. She planned to go to the grocery store to pick up a few items and then the department store and find a gift. Though Mrs. Larson would never know it, Jenna was anxious to make up for the way she had been thinking about her, and she wanted to get her something really meaningful.

Leaving the children with Nick, she drove toward the grocery store still thinking about her dream and the elderly woman. She wanted to make Mrs. Larson happy; make her feel like this last and final gift was special, something that was purchased with her specifically in mind—perhaps even a culmination of all the previous gifts.

As Jenna was driving past the grocery store on her way to the department store, she suddenly realized she needed a few additional items for dinner. Impulsively she decided to stop for just a minute before moving on to the department store. Jenna found a shopping cart just inside the doors and started pushing it toward the fruits and vegetables. As she approached the produce center she noticed a large display of Poinsettias.

The flowers were attractively arranged with white Poinsettias in the center of the display surrounded by red ones. Each potted plant was festively wrapped in red foil that was gathered together at the top with a large white ribbon. The flowers were beautiful, large and healthy.

Jenna felt inexplicably drawn to the Poinsettias. When she got to the display, suddenly her heart began to pound in her chest as a thought formed in her head: *Buy a Poinsettia for the elderly woman.*

Jenna stopped short, puzzled by the thought. *Buy a Poinsettia for the elderly woman*? Where did that come from? She smiled to herself as she wondered why in the world she would want to buy a simple grocery store Poinsettia for the elderly woman, when surely there was something bigger and better at the department store? She was anxious to make up for her bad attitude and a grocery store special just wasn't going to do it. Besides, Mrs. Larson was blind. How could she enjoy a Poinsettia? Jenna dismissed the thought and continued her grocery shopping.

After she found what she needed in the store, she headed for the checkout counter. Several customers were already in line and she had to wait a few minutes before it was her turn. While she waited, she idly read the headlines on the latest magazines. Then, from out of nowhere, the same thought as before pushed itself into the forefront of her mind: *Buy a Poinsettia for the elderly woman!*

Jenna was startled at the unexpected intrusion on her thoughts, and simultaneously realized she had that same thought when she entered the store and saw the display. How strange was that? She was about to dismiss the thought again, but something inside stopped her, and the idea began to take root. A Poinsettia? Hmm, would Mrs. Larson like a Poinsettia? Jenna finally decided she would buy the Poinsettia as a back-up gift—but if she found something better at the department store, she'd give that to Mrs. Larson instead.

Jenna excused herself from the check-out line and made her way back to the Poinsettia display. She looked at all the potted flowering plants, finally selecting a traditional red one, its leaves vibrant and strong.

As she set the Poinsettia down in her cart, a warm feeling of peace suddenly flowed over her and her heart seemed to burst with joy. She didn't know why, but any thought of buying a different gift was gone and to her surprise, she was actually excited about taking the Poinsettia to Mrs. Larson!

But at home again Jenna was having second thoughts. Especially after the way Nick looked at here when she showed him her gift.

"A Poinsettia?" he had asked in surprise. "This is what you got for the elderly lady? A flower from the grocery store?"

Jenna tried to explain how it seemed like the right thing at the time, but now she wondered if it really was. After all, it was just a flower in a pot. Why had she felt so sure about it in the store?

Jenna wondered if there was anything else she could give. Maybe something she had already purchased and wrapped for another family member?

Well, there wasn't much she could do about the Poinsettia now, she decided. Maybe it didn't matter what she gave the elderly woman. They were strangers to each other anyway. The Poinsettia was probably fine. Besides, Jenna was anxious to get the gift-giving over with so she could get back and enjoy the rest of Christmas Eve with her own family.

CHAPTER EIGHT

It was early evening when Jenna loaded the Poinsettia in the car. She rummaged through her purse to find the crumpled notecard with the address on it. Finally, after a tense moment of searching, thankfully she found the card and straightened it out so that she could see the address.

Jenna had always been terrible with directions, and even worse with numbers like street addresses. She didn't realize until she was focused on finding the elderly woman's home that she lived around the corner and eight streets up from her own home.

Jenna had fallen in love with the whole neighborhood when they were first looking for a home to buy, and she admired her surroundings again as she drove down the street. She loved the older brick homes, with their large lots and well-kept yards. Mature trees lined the street and their bare branches stretched over the road, etched white with snow against the deep blue of the evening sky.

She pulled up alongside the curb at the end of the street and looked at the address one more time. It matched the metal numbers nailed to one of the wood pillars on the front porch of the small red brick house.

Jenna's heart started pounding in her chest, and her mouth suddenly felt dry as a wave of panic came out of nowhere and washed over her. "This is crazy!" she thought. "I've been afraid of old people all my life and now I'm about to go knock on the door of one—a complete stranger—and actually give her a gift?"

Just as those thoughts entered her head, that same sweet feeling of calm reassurance she felt in the store washed over her again. Taking a deep breath, Jenna calmed herself. Even as she did, she felt a strong reassurance that she should give the Poinsettia to the woman.

The soft powdery snow muffled the sound of her footsteps as she walked around the car to retrieve the Poinsettia from the floor behind the seat. She unbuttoned her long coat and held the plant close to her chest, trying to shield it from the cold.

Jenna carefully made her way up a sidewalk that was lined with the brown withered stalks of old rose bushes protruding from drifted snow, their stalks casting eerie shadows as the night deepened. The weird shadows did nothing for the fear that was trying to bubble to the surface inside of her. Despite the calm she felt only a few moments before; she couldn't help but wonder how her gift would be received? What would she say, how would the old woman react? What if she already had a Poinsettia? Why hadn't Jenna ignored the Poinsettia and bought something else? Why had she come in the first place? ... What if the old lady was annoyed by the visit?

Just that thought alone was enough to stop Jenna in her tracks and to get her heart thumping once again. She hadn't thought about that possibility before. What would she do if Mrs. Larson was a mean old crab of a woman? Why didn't she think to get a sitter and have Nick come with her? He was so good at talking to people. With her heart now pounding in her chest, Jenna fought back the urge to bolt back to the car, toss the Poinsettia in the back, lock the doors and fly home.

Despite her desire to flee, Jenna held her ground. She took a deep breath of the cold night air to steel her nerves and to clear her head. It was now or never.

At the door, she noticed the storm door was closed, but the front door stood just barely ajar. Unsure of how well the elderly woman could hear, Jenna knocked as loudly as she could on the cold, frozen, metal door frame.

Almost immediately a rich, happy voice invited her in. Jenna didn't realize she was holding her breath till she exhaled. Well okay, that answered that question—at least Mrs. Larson didn't sound unpleasant. Maybe she could do this.

A rush of warm air greeted Jenna as she stepped from outdoors into the wood-paneled entry. Beyond it was the living room, wallpapered in a classic rose pattern. Mrs. Larson was sitting in a burgundy colored wingback chair, her back to Jenna. To Mrs. Larson's right, stacked on the sofa, was a wide array of beautiful and thoughtful gifts, obviously from Jenna's gift-giving forbearers.

There was a box of expensive chocolates, scarf and gloves, and a heating pad (of course!).

Jenna looked doubtfully at the simple, grocery store Poinsettia in her hands, and instantly felt a stab of embarrassment. Fear again filled her mind and she made a hasty decision. She decided to set the Poinsettia down behind Mrs. Larson's chair as she approached the elderly woman. She would just tell Mrs. Larson she had come to visit and then she'd take the Poinsettia home with her. Mrs. Larson would never see it.

"Uh, hi." Jenna said. "Are you Evaletta Larson?"

"Yes I am, dear. Won't you come in?" Evaletta warmly invited from her chair, motioning with her hand for Jenna to come forward. Jenna slowly walked toward her, keenly aware of the Poinsettia she carried in her arms.

"I have to apologize for not coming to the door," Evaletta said from the other side of the chair. "I lost my glasses so I am as blind as a bat—and this darned arthritis makes it hard to move! Would you please come closer so I can see you?"

Jenna hesitated only a moment to set the Poinsettia down as quietly as she could behind the chair. Then she stepped around to meet Mrs. Larson.

Mrs. Larson was a rather plump woman with rosy cheeks and a warm welcoming smile framed by rich pink lipstick. Her hair was thick and pure white and she wore it piled high in large soft swirling curls. She had on a simple blue and white flowered dress, with a white cardigan sweater draped over her shoulders and a crocheted lap quilt across her knees.

51

"What is your name, child?" Evaletta gently asked.

"Jenna," she replied, perhaps a little too fast and even a little too loud. Taking a slow breath, Jenna continued in a more carefully measured cadence, "Jenna Goodman."

"Jenna, what a beautiful name. I'm so happy to meet you. Would you please come a little closer, dear?"

"Oh, I'm . . . I'm sorry," Jenna stammered. She didn't like the idea of getting any closer, but what could she do? Jenna stepped right up to Mrs. Larson, so close, in fact that their knees were nearly touching. Jenna really was hoping that she was within Mrs. Larson's limited range of vision, because there was no way she was getting any closer.

"That's quite all right," said Evaletta. "I just like to see who it is that I am conversing with." She raised her wrinkled hands toward Jenna's face and beckoned her even closer.

Jenna groaned inside and wondered how much more she was going to have to endure before this night was over. With a mental roll of her eyes, she bent down and as she did, Mrs. Larson put her impossibly soft, warm hands on Jenna's cheeks and gently pulled her closer yet, so that now the two women's noses were nearly touching! It took every ounce of restraint Jenna had to fight the urge to pull back.

"There," Evaletta's soft voice rasped, "now I can see you. Well, aren't you pretty—and such beautiful auburn hair!"

Jenna felt color creeping to her cheeks. It wasn't

so much because of the compliment though, as it was from being so uncomfortably close to someone she didn't know.

"Thank you." Jenna said with a little self-conscious smile. At such proximity, all she could see was the pale blue of Mrs. Larson's eyes and the seemingly endless network of wrinkles, folds and creases that surrounded them.

After what seemed an eternity, Mrs. Larson's hands finally slipped from Jenna's face and nestled themselves together on the lap quilt.

With her face now free, Jenna didn't waste a moment retreating to a much more comfortable distance from the old woman. As she stepped away she breathed an almost audible sigh of relief. She wished now, more than ever before, that she would have thought to bring Nick with her.

Evaletta thoughtfully studied the shadowy form in front of her for a moment. It was hard for her to see anything, especially without her glasses. But just because her eyes didn't work like they used too, it didn't mean that her mind wasn't functioning too. Oh, it wasn't as sharp as it once was, but still not a lot got lost on her, and she chuckled to herself as she watched the young woman retreat. She determined to try to make the young woman feel as comfortable as possible.

"Please," Evaletta invited, sweeping her hand toward the sofa, "have a seat Jenna."

"Thank you." Jenna answered, trying to sound more comfortable with the situation than she obviously was.

Evaletta watched as Jenna sat down on the edge of the sofa. Just then the phone sitting on a stand at the other side of Evaletta's chair rang. The sudden sound startled the young woman and she involuntarily jumped. Evaletta decided to answer the phone and let the young woman collect herself for a moment.

Jenna was grateful for the distraction the phone call offered and she forced herself to relax a little bit. She couldn't keep her eyes from wandering to the stack of Christmas gifts on the cushion next to her: a delicate lace handkerchief with "Evaletta" stitched into it, a beautiful basket filled with soaps and lotions, an ornate musical jewelry box. She sighed as she thought how poorly her Poinsettia compared to these wonderful presents.

Mrs. Larson was still on the phone, so she took the opportunity to look around. Mrs. Larson's home was small, but comfortable. Everything was in its place, dusted and tidy. An old up-right piano filled the wall to the right of Jenna, its top covered with a yellowed, but beautiful lace runner. Pictures of family members crowded its top. A well-used reading chair upholstered in olive green crushed velvet was in a near-by corner, illuminated by an ornate metal floor lamp. A small reading table was next to it, with a large magnifying glass sitting on top of a stack of books.

Across from where Jenna sat was a large picture window, which overlooked the porch, yard and street below. The window was covered with heavy floor length rose colored drapes with precisely spaced pleats at the top.

On the wall leading into the dining room was a rather large black and white photo of a handsome smiling man. He looked like he was in his mid-forties and was wearing a suit and a loose tie. He also wore a black fedora hat, and his head was tilted up, mouth open in a laugh. His smile was charismatic and his eyes seemed to sparkle with amusement. Jenna assumed him to be Mr. Larson, and thought he looked like someone she would have liked to have known.

Jenna's eyes came back to rest on Mrs. Larson. She was talking in loving, soothing tones and there was a radiance and warmth about her that calmed Jenna and melted away some of her anxiety. Mrs. Larson seems nice enough, Jenna reassured herself. Maybe she didn't need Nick after all. To her dismay, Jenna found herself wondering if she might even enjoy spending a few minutes talking to this older woman.

Evaletta finished her conversation by announcing that she had a guest that she needed to get back to, and after expressing her love to the caller, she hung up the phone.

"You'll have to pardon me," she said apologetically, "but my children always call on Christmas Eve and I didn't want to miss one of them. I hope I didn't waste too much of your time, dear."

"Oh, no, not at all," Jenna replied, "I understand."

"Well then Jenna, why don't we get acquainted?" Evaletta asked, leaning forward in her chair.

"Okay," she agreed, feeling a little more enthusiastic about talking with Mrs. Larson than before.

"Does your family live here in Utah?"

"No" she answered, shaking her head. "My

parents still live in Oregon where I grew up."

"Oh, Oregon is so green and beautiful, isn't it!" Evaletta exclaimed.

"Yes, it is. Have you been there before?" Jenna asked, warming up to the conversation a little.

"Oh yes, we once drove up the coastline all the way from northern California to Washington. It was absolutely beautiful!" Evaletta exclaimed, obviously remembering happier times. "Is your family here for the holidays?"

"No, not for Christmas. We always get together for Thanksgiving so we don't have to travel at Christmas when the roads are bad."

"That's probably wise," Evaletta conceded. "I remember more than one harrowing Christmas trip to visit family. Every time we traveled in dangerous weather we vowed we would never do it again. But then it would be Christmas time again, and there we were, enthusiastically packing our bags!"

Jenna chuckled. "We've had a couple of trips like that, too."

"You said 'we', are you married?" Evaletta asked.

"I am," Jenna answered, smiling at the thought of Nick. If only he could see her now! He wouldn't believe it. "Nick and I have been married for almost seven years now," she said proudly. "We have two beautiful children...with another on the way," she added shyly, her hand subconsciously going to her expanded middle.

"Oh, that's wonderful!" exclaimed Evaletta. "My husband and I had three children too! A girl and two boys," she said. "In fact, that was my daughter that just called."

"Oh, what's her name?" Jenna asked.

"Lily," answered Evaletta, "after my older sister, Lillian."

"That's a beautiful name."

"Yes, it is." Lettie sighed in acknowledgment. "You know, I was always jealous of my older sister's name. It was so feminine and pretty. You couldn't help but think of soft, beautiful, things when you said "Lillian". Everyone adored her. She truly was beautiful. She was tall and willowy with ivory skin and long jet black hair. And she was as graceful as a swan." Lettie added with a smile.

"And then there was me," she exclaimed. "I was her complete opposite. I was such a tom boy! You'd sooner find me in my brother's britches scrambling up a tree than sitting on a porch like my sister all dressed up in ribbons and sashes and sipping lemonade! No one could ever believe we were sisters. Not only did I have the most cumbersome name in the world—"Evaletta" doesn't exactly roll off the tongue—but I was a squat, round little thing with blotchy freckles from my nose to my ankles and hair about as appealing as a pile of dirt . . . come to think of it, it really was the color of dirt!" Lettie laughed merrily.

Jenna couldn't help but laugh with her.

"Oh, but there I go rambling on about myself!" Evaletta suddenly exclaimed in dismay.

"You're fine," Jenna laughed, "I enjoyed listening to you."

"Well, thank you." Responded Evaletta with a

gracious nod of her head, "but let's talk about you now," she said with a smile. "Do you work?"

"Yes, at home as a freelance writer."

"Oh, that's wonderful! And what do you write?"

"Oh," Jenna shrugged her shoulders, "mostly marketing content for on-line companies." She explained as simply as she could, unsure how much Mrs. Larson knew about the Web.

"Goodness!" exclaimed the elderly woman, "that must be demanding with a young family to care for."

"It can be," Jenna acknowledged, "but it is satisfying to have a creative outlet."

"I think I know what you mean." Evaletta said, finding some common ground with the young woman in her living room. Then leaning forward in her chair, she continued. "Did you know I was about your age when I had my first poem published?"

Jenna was impressed. "You write poetry?"

"Why, yes, I do—or at least I did until these old eyes gave out on me," Evaletta said with a conspiratorial wink. "But that first poem...Oh, I was so excited!" she exclaimed, softly clapping her hands together. "It was just a little children's rhyme, a ditty really, that was part of a collection for a book that became very popular. You see, this was during the Great Depression, and money was tight for us, like it was for a lot of folks." Evaletta explained. "I had been praying that somehow I could find a way to bring in some additional income to help my husband provide for our little family. Then one day I saw an advertisement in a magazine. It was asking for submissions of original poetry. I had always enjoyed writing poetry and so I took a chance and sent one of my poems in—and they accepted it. I really felt my prayers had been answered. It wasn't a lot of money, mind you," Evaletta confided, "but it was enough to help us get by for a while. Oh, I was so grateful." She said, her head bobbing up and down in confirmation of her words. Evaletta paused for a few moments, apparently lost in her thoughts. Then she continued in a quiet tone, almost to herself, "God loves us. I know he hears our prayers. He may not always answer them when or how we might think He should, but I do know that He hears us, and sooner or later, he does answer."

Jenna nodded her head appreciatively. It seemed she had more experience with those "later" answers than the "sooner" ones. Take her desire to feel the Christmas Spirit...It was certainly late in coming. Very late. Rather than think too much about it, she decided to change the subject.

"What poem did you write?" Jenna asked, curious now about the elderly woman in front of her.

Evaletta looked up from her reverie in surprise. "Oh, I'm sorry. Did you ask about my poem?"

"Yes," Jenna smiled. "I was wondering what poem you wrote."

"Oh dear! You don't want to hear that old thing!" Evaletta exclaimed, swatting the air dismissively.

"Yes, I do. Please tell me," she coaxed.

"Well, all right then." Evaletta said, settled back into her chair. She paused for a moment and then began. "It's called Mrs. Mahitty. It goes like this:

"Mrs. Mahitty had a kitty.
She named him Kitty-poo.
But he was black,
and she couldn't have that,
for a black cat wouldn't do.
So late one night she painted him white,
and thought no one could tell.
But the very next day
when he went out to play—"

Just as Mrs. Larson was about to finish the verse, Jenna joined in to recite it with her: *"he got spots when the raindrops fell!"* They finished in unison.

"You know my poem?" Evaletta asked in astonishment.

Jenna started laughing. "I do! I learned it when I was little. I can't believe that you wrote it!" she exclaimed. "I've always loved that rhyme."

The rest of the evening was spent in pleasant conversation, punctuated with laughter. Glancing at her watch, Jenna was surprised at how quickly the time had passed. In fact, she had been enjoying her conversation with Mrs. Larson so much that she had forgotten the reason she was there in the first place. Jenna got up to leave and was about to say her good-byes, when she saw the hidden Poinsettia.

Suddenly it felt as if butterflies took flight in Jenna's tummy and her throat went dry. She wanted to give the Poinsettia to Mrs. Larson, but how? She felt reasonably assured that she would accept any-thing with appreciation, and so Jenna decided to just jump in. "Mrs. Larson," she began, "I—"

"Please," interjected the elderly woman, "my friends call me Lettie."

Jenna smiled at the inference that she was her friend. She was pretty sure Lettie was hers. "Okay, Lettie," she began again. "I've enjoyed talking with you so much that I forgot the reason I came to visit you tonight."

"Oh?"

"I brought you a gift for the Twelfth Day of Christmas." Jenna explained.

"You brought me a gift? How sweet of you!" Lettie exclaimed. Her eyes seemed to light up in anticipation, reminding Jenna of the look on her own children's faces on Christmas morning. She sincerely hoped Lettie wouldn't be too disappointed. It was after all, just a simple Poinsettia.

"I've never enjoyed so much company and so many thoughtful gifts as I have over these past several days" Lettie said, her face radiating her happiness.

Jenna stepped around Lettie's chair and retrieved the Poinsettia. Compared with the other gifts Lettie had received, the Poinsettia seemed overly simple. "It's not much," Jenna said apologetically as she placed the potted plant on Lettie's lap. Lettie wrapped her hands around the foil, exploring the texture.

"What is it?" she asked.

"It's a Poinsettia," Jenna answered sheepishly. Then, to her astonishment, Lettie's face froze in shocked disbelief. Jenna's heart sank at Lettie's reaction to the Poinsettia and a million thoughts ran through her mind in that moment—most of them having to do with the absurdity of giving a Poinsettia to a blind woman. She should have known better. Why had she thought this was a good idea? Her heart began to pound and she felt her cheeks flush with color.

Then, to Jenna's further surprise, Lettie pulled the Poinsettia tightly to her chest. Jenna watched in bewilderment as large tears filled Lettie's eyes and spilled down her wrinkled cheeks. Lettie began to gently rock back and forth, her arms wrapped tightly around the Poinsettia. "Oh Sweetheart!" she wept as she rocked. "My darling. I've missed you so much! I love you too!"

Jenna waited quietly, too baffled to know what else to do. After a minute or two, Lettie's weeping subsided. She carefully set the Poinsettia on the end table and dabbed at her eyes with a tissue she produced from her dress pocket. Another moment passed as she composed herself, and then she smiled at Jenna, warm and radiant through her tears.

"I'm sorry," she whispered. "I didn't mean to blubber like a baby, but your gift caught me off-guard."

"I—I guess I don't understand," Jenna hesitantly replied.

Lettie drew in a deep, steadying breath. Her eyes were still wet; her emotions still close to the surface. "Let me explain," she offered. "My husband—my dear Richard—died three years ago" she began in a quivering voice. Lettie pursed her lips together and drew in another breath as she looked toward the black and white photo of him on the wall. "I can't tell you how much I miss him," she continued, trying to hold back fresh tears. "I have felt so alone." Lettie whispered in a voice cracking with emotion, her wet eyes downcast. She slowly shook her head. "He was the love of my life...The most wonderful man in the whole world. We shared every day together from sun up to sun down for over six decades. It never occurred to me that he might die one day and leave me to face life alone."

Jenna felt tears jump to her own eyes as compassion for Lettie welled up inside her. Jenna knelt at Lettie's side and put her hand on her knee to comfort her.

"I just want to hold him again," Lettie whispered, as fresh tears found their way down her wrinkled cheeks. Then Lettie wiped her eyes and cleared her throat and straightened up a bit in her chair. "I have been praying for a long, long time," she said in a stronger voice, "that God would give me one last blessing: I've been asking Him if He could somehow let me know that my Richard misses me as much as I miss him, and that he still thinks about me and—and that he still loves me. And tonight," Lettie said, her face breaking into a radiant smile, "He answered my prayers and sent you!"

"Me?" Jenna repeated in surprise. "I don't understand! How am I an answer to your prayers?"

Lettie became somber for a moment. A faraway look came to her eyes and sadness settled over her face. She gave Jenna's hand a small squeeze and began, "You didn't know this, but today would have been our sixty-fifth wedding anniversary," she whispered. "When Richard and I celebrated our first anniversary, he gave me a Poinsettia. I didn't think too much about it, except that I thought it was a sweet gesture. Then he gave me a Poinsettia on our second anniversary." Lettie's eyes misted over again for a moment, but she continued. "When he gave the second Poinsettia, I asked him why. Do you know what he said?"

"No," Jenna answered, "what?"

"He said, 'Because the Poinsettia symbolizes enduring love, and I have always loved you Evaletta Larson, and I will love you forever'—that was his answer! I looked forward to getting a Poinsettia on our anniversary from him every year after that."

Lettie looked at Jenna and smiled as tears found their way down her cheeks again. "And through you, God has shown me that Richard still loves me."

Jenna looked from Lettie to the Poinsettia in stunned realization. No wonder she had felt so strongly about buying the Poinsettia! As she gazed at the potted plant, it seemed to change right before her eyes. Instead of a simple festive department store plant, she saw an amazingly beautiful flower that had become a symbol of eternal love between an adoring husband and his beloved wife. He had loved her with all of his heart in life and was now telling her that he continued to love her even after death!

Jenna blinked back tears that were gathering in her eyes as Lettie continued. "I haven't had a Poinsettia since he died three years ago." She said quietly. "Not until tonight. Thank you, Jenna, for being an answer to the prayers of an old woman."

Tears spilled from Jenna's eyes as she humbly considered her part in God's plan for Lettie's happiness. "Oh, Lettie!" she cried, "I'm so happy for you!"

And truly she was. Jenna's heart felt like it was going to burst with pure joy as the Spirit of Christmas—the Holy Spirit of God—infused her soul with warmth and indescribable joy. She couldn't believe it! It was all so amazing to her: God knew what Lettie needed and He knew what Jenna needed, and He had prepared a way for both of their prayers to be answered.

A few minutes later, Jenna warmly wished Lettie a Merry Christmas and left her with the promise that she would return again soon.

As Jenna walked to her car, she stopped for a moment to look up at the night sky. The stars looked just a little closer and brighter than they did when she'd fearfully walked to Lettie's door earlier that evening. The joy she felt now—that both she and Lettie shared that evening—still lingered in her soul and she couldn't help but smile as she looked up into that beautiful heavenly expanse. "Thank you." she whispered. "Thank you so much!"

EPILOGUE

Lettie died in early December a year later. The days that followed her death were difficult for Jenna. She nursed the ache in her heart for the loss of her dear friend as best she could, but she often found herself just going through the motions of the day, wrapped up in the tapestry of memories Lettie and she had woven together in the short year they'd known each other: the visits, the outings, the laughter, her love of life and warmth of spirit, and her advice—how was she going to live without her? How were Nick and her three children going to get along without "Grandma L"? She had truly become a part of their family and she'd come to dearly love the only "grandmother" she had ever known.

Lettie's funeral was simple and beautiful, just like her life had been. Jenna was determined not to cry at the service, but her reserve fled when Lettie's oldest son eulogized his mother's tender and loving care with the familiar poem by Margaret Widener:

She always leaned to watch for us,
Anxious if we were late,
In winter by the window,
In summer by the gate;

And though we mocked her tenderly,
Who had such foolish care,
The long way home would seem more safe
Because she waited there.

Her thoughts were all so full of us,
She never could forget!
And so I think that where she is
She must be watching yet,

Waiting till we come home to her,
Anxious if we are late.
Watching from Heaven's window
Leaning from Heaven's gate.

Jenna couldn't help but quietly weep when she thought of how often Lettie had demonstrated that kind of love to her and her own little family.

And then again, she found herself blinking back tears as she watched Lettie's children gather around the open casket to lovingly caress their mother's hands and tenderly kiss her soft cheeks one last time. Jenna knew the sorrow reflected in each of their faces was also on hers when she took her turn at the casket.

"Oh, Lettie," Jenna said softly, "I miss you so much!" Tears found their way down her cheeks as she continued. "Thank you, so much, for all you have done for me and for my family." Jenna squeezed Lettie's hand as she looked at her dear friend one last time. She knew she should say her final goodbye, so wiping her eyes and taking a deep, steadying breath, Jenna whispered, "Lettie, I brought you a beautiful red Poinsettia. It's out in the foyer with all the other flowers. I've never forgotten what Richard said about them. He said 'Poinsettias symbolize enduring love.' I want you to know I love you, Evaletta Larson, and I will love you forever."

Made in the USA
Monee, IL
16 December 2019

18765541R00039